Let's go to Mass

Text by Fr Paul Maddison

Illustrations by
Jennifer Carter

W0006906

are getting out of bed

and making their way

to church.

Mass normally starts with a hymn or song,
then we make the sign of the cross to remind us
that we love God, are friends of Jesus and are
filled with the Holy Spirit.

We say:
In the name of the Father,
and of the Son,
and of the Holy Spirit.
Amen.

The priest welcomes us and
asks us to get ready to worship God
by being sorry for our sins,
for the times we have not done
what God would want us to do.

Perhaps you can think of something
that you would want to say sorry
to God for. You could ask yourself:
have I been rude or spiteful,
have I not shared things,
have I told lies or been unkind?

Why not ask God to help you
be kinder during the next week?

We say the 'Gloria', the prayer of the angels at the birth of Jesus in Bethlehem.

We bless you, we praise you, we thank you!

The priest prays for us to God.

We don't have any photos of Jesus, or his disciples. We don't have photos of people like Moses or Abraham, so to help us get to know them we listen to readings from our history, the Bible.

We learn that Jesus was kind and good, that St Paul went on many journeys telling people about Jesus; we learn that Abraham loved God, that Moses freed the people of Israel from Egypt.

How many people in our picture do you know something about?

The priest talks to us about the readings we have heard. This is called the 'homily'. It helps to show us how we can become more like Jesus, the Son of God.

When the priest stands up you will be able to see the colour of his vestments. White for wonderful feasts like Christmas and Easter, purple for sorry times like Lent and funerals; red to remind us of the Holy Spirit or the saints who died for Jesus; and green to remind us of the glorious world that God has created for us.

What colour is the priest wearing today?

We stand to say the Creed – the prayer which tells everyone what we believe.

We believe in God our Father, who made the world in which we live.

We believe in Jesus Christ, the Son of God. He was born by the power of the Holy Spirit and Mary was his mother. Jesus was crucified and died for us, but after three days he rose from the dead. Jesus returned to heaven and lives with God and one day he will come again.

We believe in the Holy Spirit who helps us all to live like Jesus.

We believe in the Church where we are all one family.

Amen.

You can tell people how you believe in God by doing good things at home or in school, by sharing and being kind.

The priest invites us to pray to God for the things we need.

We pray for his church,
for the people who have no homes,
who do not have enough to eat,
or are unhappy.
We pray for ourselves;
for the sick
and for those who have died.

Perhaps you can make up a prayer
in your heart asking God to care for
someone you know.

At the end of these prayers we
ask Mary, the mother of Jesus,
to pray with us.

We sing another hymn now while the collection is taken.

Years ago, when the church first began to celebrate Mass, people would bring chickens, blankets, bread and lots of other 'gifts' to Mass. These would be collected and given out to the poor people at the end of Mass.

Can you see the lady bringing the loaf of bread to offer to God?

Today we give money to help pay for all the work that the church does around the world, like caring for the poor, helping to run our schools, giving food to the hungry and so on.

The bread and wine are brought to the priest along with the collection.

Perhaps you can say a little prayer in your heart to offer yourself: Jesus, help me to do things for you. Use me to tell others how good you are. Amen.

The priest asks us to pray and we stand.
He reminds us how good God is and asks
us to 'lift up our hearts'.

St John, who was a special friend of Jesus,
had a dream in which he saw all the
angels and saints in heaven singing a great
prayer. We join with them as we pray:

Holy, holy, holy Lord,
God of power and might.
Heaven and earth are full of your glory.
Hosanna in the highest.
Blessed is he who comes
in the name of the Lord.
Hosanna in the highest.

We now kneel while the priest says the great prayer of thanksgiving called the 'Eucharistic Prayer'.

If you listen carefully you will hear him pray for the church, for our Pope and for the bishop. He will pray for the Holy Spirit to come down from heaven to change the bread and wine into the body and blood of Christ.

He will say the words that Jesus said at the Last Supper on the night before he died:

Take this all of you and eat it,
this is my body which will be given for you.

After this the priest genuflects; we bow our heads as a mark of respect to Jesus.

Take this all of you and drink from it,
this is the cup of my blood,
the blood of the new and everlasting covenant.
It will be shed for you and for all
so that sins may be forgiven.
Do this in memory of me.

Again we bow our heads, thinking of
how much Jesus loved us to die for us.

The priest carries on with the prayer, remembering the saints: perhaps if it is a special day he will mention their name. He also prays for those who have died. Pray for them now.

In Jerusalem there is a church on the spot where Jesus is said to have taught his friends the 'Our Father'. Around the walls of that church the prayer is written in nearly every language of the world.

We stand to say that prayer now, the prayer that is known throughout the world:

Our Father, who art in heaven,
hallowed be thy name.
Thy kingdom come,
thy will be done
on earth as it is in heaven.
Give us this day our daily bread
and forgive our trespasses
as we forgive those
who trespass against us.
And lead us not into temptation
but deliver us from evil.
Amen.

Jesus asked us to be people of peace
and before he is given in communion
we should be friends with one another.

The priest asks us to offer each other a
sign of peace. We shake hands or give
a kiss to show that we are all friends.

As people go to communion they become very close to Jesus. They want to pray and tell him how much they love him. To help them it is usually quiet now, or a gentle hymn is sung.

If you go to communion remember to tell Jesus how much you love him.

If you have not made your First Communion yet, ask the priest to bless you.

At the end of the Mass the priest gives God's blessing and sends us out into the world to bring the love and joy of Jesus into the lives of the people we meet.

We can care like Jesus did, we can forgive people like he did, we can share with others, be friends and love like Jesus did.

Can you see the people being kind in these pictures?

Notes for parents

Keeping a child's attention is never easy! This book aims to provide some assistance in the very necessary task parents face in helping their children to appreciate the Mass.

The Mass has, as its final act, the sending out of the congregation 'to love and serve the Lord'. Hopefully this book will enable that to become a reality in the lives of our young people.

For Eleanor

First published in 1994 by
KEVIN MAYHEW LTD
Rattlesden
Bury St Edmunds
Suffolk IP30 0SZ

ISBN 0 86209 546 8
Catalogue No 1500009

Printed in Great Britain